Dr l
Thanks for
all you do!

IN THE
Shadow
OF THE CROSS

Stephanie K Adams
Matt 16:24

STEPHANIE K. ADAMS

In the Shadow of the Cross, paints a vivid picture for readers and invites them to lean in close during such a pivotal time in Christianity—our Savior's last days. Key moments come alive through beautiful storytelling as you imagine the weight of every sacrifice that leads Jesus to the cross. I love how Stephanie leads you in prayer, deeper in studying scriptures, and then provides personal application. I highly recommend savoring each page in reflection and falling in love with Jesus all over again.

- **Jennifer Renee Watson**, author of
Freedom!: The Gutsy Pursuit of Breakthrough and the Life Beyond It

Stephanie has put together a beautiful devotional that walks through Jesus' final days on earth leading up to the cross. In this devotional study of *In the Shadow of the Cross* we find hope, help, and a heart-throbbing remembrance of the Savior. It's beautiful! My heart was convicted and comforted and I know yours will be too!

- **Micah Maddox** - Women's Conference Speaker and Author of
Anchored In: Experience a Power-Full Life in a Problem-Filled World

Jesus is the way. A great opportunity lays before us to find our way, in Him. The devotional book, *In The Shadow of The Cross*, will guide you deeper into Christ's heart so that you can live with more freedom, purpose and life.

- **Kelly Balarie**, Blogger, Speaker and Author of
Fear Fighting: Awakening Courage to Overcome Your Fears and
Battle Ready: Train your Mind to Conquer Challenges, Defeat Doubt and Live Victoriously

What an incredible resource and in-depth look at the final days of Jesus Christ during His time here on Earth. From the prayer prompts, to the word studies, to the suggested additional reading, *In the Shadow of the Cross* helped me catch a fresh glimpse of those final days. I have a renewed perspective on the incredible details of that week and the powerful and profound effect those final days have on my everyday life.

> - **Kristin Funston**, Bible teacher, speaker, ministry leader, and author of *More for Mom: Living Your Whole & Holy Life*

In the Shadow of the Cross invites the reader to take Jesus' last steps toward the cross with Him and compels the reader to go deeper in thought with insightful questions. The reader will trace Jesus' final hours as seen through the eyes of each gospel writer and be inspired to see Him through their own as they are encouraged to walk closer with Christ. *In the Shadow of the Cross* is a must-have for anyone desiring a closer walk with Jesus. Stephanie invites us on a journey and then gives us what we need the most, a map! This guide is perfect for time alone or with a group.

> - **Jodie Barrett**, co-founder of Faithfully Following Ministries, Bible teacher, and author of *Jingle and Joy: Praying Beneath the Tree*

Stephanie provides a fresh perspective about the last days of Jesus' life. This study pinpoints the pivotal moments surrounding, and leading up to, the crucifixion. Her writing is honest, relevant, and will speak to the heart of today's Christian woman. *In the Shadow of the Cross* is a perfect study for women across the generations.

> - **Mitzi Neely,** Peacefully Imperfect Ministries, Author of *A Thankful Heart* and *Dwell in the Psalms*.

Contents

Introduction

For the past few years I have spent time reading and meditating on the Scriptures surrounding the last days of Christ's life before His crucifixion.

When I first compiled a Scripture reading list my goal was to focus on the events surrounding what we celebrate as the Easter season. What I actually found was a closer, deeper relationship with Jesus as I began imagining what it must have been like for Him to walk those last days with the shadow of the cross looming over Him. Every event that takes place, every word spoken, the cross is waiting at the end for Jesus.

That's how the name of this devotional study, *In the Shadow of the Cross*, was born.

As I read I asked myself questions—how would I react if I were there? If I heard the words Jesus said? Experienced what the disciples were witnessing? Watched the events unfolding right before my very eyes?

I began to record my thoughts and soon, what started as a simple reading list, ended up being a collection of devotions and thought-provoking questions as I followed Christ through His last days.

Each day as you read through Scripture from the Gospels of Matthew, Mark, Luke, and/or John, imagine yourself present in the moment with Jesus and His disciples. Listen in as they speak. Look around and see what is happening as Jesus approaches the cross and the darkness grows. Picture yourself there and imagine your own reactions to the events.

Each day's focus is a small window into a specific event during Jesus' last week before the cross. You will find verses to read, a devotional to guide your thoughts, and a *Looking Beyond* section for those who desire an even deeper understanding of the Scripture.

I encourage you to read the verses listed in the *Second Glance* section. These will give you a broader perspective of the events and expand upon what Jesus has to say to us.

The content of the study is not a full discussion of every possible lesson/life application contained in the Scriptures. You may find God will speak something new and fresh to you from the content in the book. Do not hesitate to journal what He teaches you through these Scriptures.

It is my prayer that as you journey through these 21-days of Scripture, you will find yourself growing closer to Jesus and falling in love with Him all over again...or maybe even for the first time.

Stephanie K. Adams

day one

FOLLOW ME

"Then Jesus said to His disciples, 'If anyone wishes to come after Me, he must deny himself, and take up his cross and follow Me. For whoever wishes to save his life will lose it; but whoever loses his life for My sake will find it.'" Matthew 16:24-25

As we begin our journey in the shadow of the cross, let's prepare our hearts by looking at an important requirement for following after Jesus—a willingness to sacrifice.

This is exactly what Christ did for us—He willingly gave up His own life so we can have eternal life. He was the sacrifice God required for our sins to be forgiven once and for all.

Denying yourself is a refining process meant to draw you closer to Jesus and make you more like Him

In turn, He says if we are to follow Him as believers we must also be willing to sacrifice.

But what is sacrifice? Sacrifice is giving up something as an offering; the giving up of one thing for another.

Following after Jesus as a believer demands you must also give up your own desires to pursue His plans for your everyday life. Likewise, preparing your heart to journey through 21 days of Scripture involves letting go of some things in order to remain focused.

Distraction is one of the top reasons for being frustrated with Bible study and prayer—and it is almost certain to occur.

As you stand in the shadow of the cross, watching Christ in His last days, what is God asking you to give up during the next 21 days to remain dedicated to prayer and Scripture?

Jesus, as I journey through Scripture over the next few weeks, help me to slow my pace as I seek to learn from Your last days before the cross. Help me to follow after You. Show me the things in my life that hinder me from experiencing You fully. I devote this time to focus on the sacrifice of the cross and recommit to following You. In Jesus' name. Amen.

Second Glance: Mark 8:34-35; Luke 9:23-24; 2 Timothy 2:11-13; Titus 2:12

Looking Beyond

Let's take a deeper look at the meaning of the word *deny* when Jesus said, *"If anyone would come after me, let him deny himself..."*

The Greek word for *deny* is *Aparneomai [ap-ar-neh'-om-ahee]*, which means to *affirm that one has no acquaintance or connection with someone, to forget one's self, lose sight of one's self and one's own interests.*

Apameomai is from the root word *Apo [apo']* which means *separation*. It is also from the root word *Arneomai [ar-neh'-om-ahee]* which means *to disregard one's own interests and to act entirely unlike oneself.*

Jesus is asking us to separate ourselves from the world, and its distractions, and to join with Him by following His example.

Taking up your cross is symbolic for sacrifice, and a sacrifice requires something to die. In this case, the death is your desires—giving up your expectations to embrace God's plans for your life. Denying yourself is a refining process meant to draw you closer to Jesus and make you more like Him.

During this refining process, Jesus will begin to show you things that keep you from going deeper and getting closer.

There are a lot of things you can do to stay focused during this 21-day journey through Scripture. This is a great time to evaluate how and with whom you spend your time and energy and consider making some changes for the better.

Using your time wisely is the best way to make sure you have time in His Word every day. This could mean taking a break from social media, television, or anything else that distracts you from focusing on Scripture and prayer.

Sometimes having friends to encourage you to pursue Jesus and His Word or pray with/for you helps you stay motivated. Invite a friend or two to do this study with you or host a small group study in your home or church.

What are some other things you can do to pursue a life of following Jesus? Is He asking you to give up something? Maybe He's asking you to begin doing something for Him?

Spend time in prayer then journal your thoughts.

ANOINTED AT BETHANY

"Jesus, therefore, six days before the Passover, came to Bethany where Lazarus was, whom Jesus had raised from the dead. So they made Him a supper there, and Martha was serving; but Lazarus was one of those reclining at the table with Him. Mary then took a pound of very costly perfume of pure nard, and anointed the feet of Jesus and wiped His feet with her hair; and the house was filled with the fragrance of the perfume. But Judas Iscariot, one of His disciples, who was intending to betray Him, said, 'Why was this perfume not sold for three hundred denarii and given to poor people?' Now he said this, not because he was concerned about the poor, but because he was a thief, and as he had the money box, he used to pilfer what was put into it. Therefore Jesus said, 'Let her alone, so that she may keep it for the day of My burial. For you always have the poor with you, but you do not always have Me.'" John 12:1-8

Imagine yourself sitting at the dinner table with your closest friends. Suddenly an aromatic fragrance fills the air and before you can identify it you realize a woman is anointing the feet of Jesus.

Her unhindered worship mingles with the perfume and fills the room with love for her Savior. She is not distracted by the presence of others in the room. She is not moved by the condemning conversation surrounding her. She is focused in worship. The only words she hears are those spoken by the object of her worship:

"...she has done a beautiful thing to me."
Matthew 26:10 ESV

When we come to God in authentic worship, unhindered by our surroundings, our spirit lingers in His presence—and it is a beautiful thing—a sweet fragrance to Jesus.

Over the next weeks we will be watching as Christ prepares for His final days before the crucifixion. May we spend time in prayer and worship, meditating on the sacrifice He made so we can come into His presence and have a relationship with Him.

Jesus, help me to focus on You this week. Remind me of all the ways You suffered for me—not just physically, but also emotionally, as You carried the weight of the knowledge of what was to come. Help me to see myself walking these last days beside You. Show me this last week in a fresh, new perspective, making it more real to me. In Jesus' name. Amen.

Second Glance: Matthew 26:6-13; Mark 14:3-9

Looking Beyond

The ointment of nard (also called Spikenard) was used in ancient times to anoint the head of someone of great wealth and authority. It was highly valued and considered the very best someone could give.

Nard was not only used to anoint, but also as an anti-bacterial ointment for infections on the skin and because its fragrance is strong and lingers for quite some time, it was considered calming and effective for relieving stress.

When Mary used the expensive perfume to anoint Jesus, it was possibly the only thing of value she owned, indicating her desire to give sacrificially to the Lord. And her worship cost her not only in possession and money, but it could have also cost her reputation as she performed this most intimate act of worship in a room full of men, who clearly objected to what took place. In a time when women were not valued as they are now, it would have been scandalous for a woman to presume to place herself in the presence of the men, let alone touch one they called Teacher.

When Jesus corrects them saying, *"Let her alone, so that she may keep it for the day of My burial,"* He uses the Greek word for *burial*, which is *Entaphiasmos [en-taf-ee-as-mos']* meaning *preparation of a body for burial.*

Jesus understands the events He faces in the coming days will be brutal and violent and lead to His death. Mary's worship was a gift to Jesus in a way only He could fully appreciate in that moment.

Jesus acknowledges Mary is preparing His body for death, but perhaps He also knows the ointment will help when the whip tears into His flesh, or the fragrance will linger long enough to remind Him of why He's enduring such torture.

Mary is not only preparing Jesus, she is also creating a special memory *"that she may keep"* to sustain her during one of the darkest times she will face.

When we worship God, giving Him all we have, not worrying who is watching or what they will say, but instead focus completely on Jesus, we not only show our love to Him, but we also create remembrances to strengthen our spirits to face dark days.

Today as you take a *Second Glance*, spend time listing ways you can incorporate worship throughout this study. You could listen to worship music while you pray, or maybe instead you need to find a quiet, special place to help you focus. What are some other ways you can think of to add worship to your study time?

ENTRY TO JERUSALEM

"The disciples went and did just as Jesus had instructed them, and brought the donkey and the colt, and laid their coats on them; and He sat on the coats. Most of the crowd spread their coats in the road, and others were cutting branches from the trees and spreading them in the road. The crowds going ahead of Him, and those who followed, were shouting, 'Hosanna to the Son of David; Blessed is He who comes in the name of the Lord; Hosanna in the highest!'"
Matthew 21:6-9

The streets are crowded as visitors gather into the city for the Passover feast. Through the noise and congestion, as families and friends greet each other, children run and laugh, two young men struggle to lead a new colt through the streets.

Hosanna! Blessed is He who comes in the name of the Lord!

The crowd begins to whisper—
"It's Him."
"That's Jesus, the One who brought Lazarus back from the dead."
"Did you hear He healed the blind man?"

Suddenly, men begin cutting palm branches and passing them around. The crowd begins to cry out, *"Hosanna! Blessed is He who comes in the name of the Lord!"* as they spread their coats on the ground for the man sitting atop the donkey.

Finally, the Messiah has arrived!

However, as we will soon find out, the people did not see Jesus for who He really was—the Christ—instead they placed their personal expectations on Him. They were looking for someone to liberate them from Rome and their oppressive rule. They didn't understand

Christ came to establish a Heavenly Kingdom. They didn't realize His mission wasn't to bring about the temporary peace they wanted but to provide them with an eternal security only His salvation could bring.

As you watch the joyful crowd praising Jesus, ask yourself who Jesus is to you. Is He someone you hope will meet your expectations? Do you look to Him only for your temporary needs? Or do you see Him as your Savior, the one who gave His life to save you from your sins and has His own plans for you?

Jesus, forgive me when I have tried to make You into someone or something You are not. Help me to remember the sacrifice You gave to bring me into relationship with You. Thank You, Lord, for being my Savior. Help me to seek Your plans, instead of placing my expectations on You. In Jesus' name. Amen.

Second Glance: Matthew 21:1-11; Mark 11:1-10; Luke 19:28-40; John 12:12-15

Looking Beyond

Jesus' entry into Jerusalem, which we commemorate on Palm Sunday, happened approximately one week before His crucifixion. Jesus had been making this same trip to Jerusalem for Passover every year since he was 12 years old, as Mary and Joseph were faithful to observe the Jewish customs.

"Now His parents went to Jerusalem every year at the Feast of the Passover. And when He became twelve, they went up there according to the custom of the Feast." Luke 2:41-42

Jesus was no stranger to the Temple or the priests. He took advantage of His time in the city to learn and teach, even as a young boy.

"Then, after three days they found Him in the temple, sitting in the midst of the teachers, both listening to them and asking them questions. And all who heard Him were amazed at His understanding and His answers." Luke 2:46-47

He has spent the last several years visiting town after town teaching and performing miracles, always coming back here to keep the customs of His people, but this will be His last journey to Jerusalem for Passover.

As He arrives, the crowd cries out, *"Hosanna,"* which comes from the Greek *Yasha`* [yaw-shah'] meaning *to save, be delivered*; and *Na'* [naw] meaning *an exclamation of praise, adoration*.

They openly praise God for sending their Savior to deliver them. No doubt the people have heard of the miracles, especially regarding Lazarus, and they believe Jesus to be the promised Messiah. While Jesus certainly performed miracles in a physical sense as prophesied, the people fail to see the spiritual reality of their need.

And although Jesus knows their praise will quickly turn into anger as their earthly expectations of Him go unmet, He quietly rides through town accepting the praise of the people He deeply loves.

This is going to be a long, dark week for Jesus, and for us, as we follow along, quietly lingering in the shadow cast by the cross looming over the events of the week.

There will be joy and there will tears. But, don't turn back. Keep following after Jesus—all the way to the foot of the cross.

Today, let's celebrate Jesus, the Messiah—the One who saves!

Write a prayer of Hosanna—praise and adoration. List all the ways Jesus has delivered and saved you, both physically and spiritually, and then give Him praise.

day four
JESUS WEEPS

"When He approached Jerusalem, He saw the city and wept over it, saying, 'If you had known in this day, even you, the things which make for peace! But now they have been hidden from your eyes.'"
Luke 19:41-42

Today we stand and watch as Jesus prepares for His last days. Looking out over Jerusalem with a heavy heart, He begins to weep bitterly because His chosen people Israel, the very ones for whom He will soon embrace the cross, have rejected Him. They do not recognize Him as their Messiah, their Savior, their King.

Because they refuse to acknowledge Him and accept His sacrifice in exchange for their salvation, Christ knows the future will bring hard times for Jerusalem—and it grieves His soul. Ultimately, He knows their refusal of Him as Savior won't just bring destruction to them as a nation, but will also cost them eternity with Him.

Jesus, thank you for loving me enough to embrace the cross

As you stand in the shadow of the cross, looking up to where Christ will die for you, do you acknowledge Him?

Is He your Savior—the redeemer of your soul?
Is He your Messiah—the anointed one, Lord of your life?

If not, can I share with you that Jesus weeps for you, too. He wants you to know your physical death on earth is not the end, and you can live forever with Him in heaven.

He wants to not only rescue you from eternal death, but He wants to be your Helper through life's difficult times and the source of your joy. He longs to be part of every aspect of your life.

Unlike those in Jerusalem that day, we as Christians do identify Christ as the Messiah, but we are often guilty of failing to acknowledge Him in different ways. We allow daily distractions to take our focus off of His goodness and blessings. We become so busy we fail to spend time with Him in prayer. When hard times come, we lose sight of the fact that He's right beside us, listening to every prayer, watching out for our every need.

Can I tell you when we forget He's there, waiting for us to reach for Him, His heart breaks over us, too.

Before you continue journeying through Jesus' last days before the cross, it's important to pause and evaluate your relationship with Jesus.

First and foremost, do you know Him as your Savior? If not, you can ask Him for His gift of salvation today. It is my prayer if you are reading this and don't already know Jesus as Savior, you would ask for the free gift of His salvation and begin a relationship with Him today.

Next, spend time in prayer asking Him to remind you of all the ways He has met you in your daily routine—whether physical, financial, emotional, etc.—and then take a moment to acknowledge Him with a prayer of thanks.

Finally, consider any hardships you are currently facing and ask Him to show you how you can cast your cares on Him and usher in His peace.

Jesus, thank You for loving me enough to embrace the cross. Thank You for walking with me throughout my busy week. Help me to acknowledge You, to make You the first place I turn when my life gets hectic. Teach me how to trust You with all the details weighing heavily on my heart. Help me recognize Your presence as I go about my day. In Jesus' name. Amen.

Second Glance: Luke 19:41-44

Looking Beyond

Today's key verse says Jesus wept over Jerusalem. The Greek word for *wept* is *Klaio [klah'-yo]*, which means *to mourn, or weep as the sign of pain and grief, mourn for, and bewail (great bitterness)*.

This isn't just a quiet shedding of tears. This is a gut-wrenching, bitter moaning over the eternal death of God's beloved children. Jesus is deeply distressed over those who do not accept His gift of salvation.

His heart cry is that everyone would know "the things that make for peace."

The Greek word for *peace* in this verse is *Eirene [i-ray'nay]* which at first glance does indeed mean *exemption from war*, but it also has the *meaning of security, safety, and even "the Messiah's peace—the way that leads to salvation."*

Jesus' bitter weeping was because He desperately wanted Jerusalem, and us, to know Him as the Peace-giver.

When was the last time you felt a true sense of peace in the midst of hard circumstances? Maybe you're grieving over the loss of a loved one who has passed, or a marriage, or job. Maybe you are facing a health diagnosis that feels pretty hopeless. Or possibly you are praying earnestly for someone who is unsaved—perhaps your own children. Whatever circumstances you are facing, Jesus wants you to know "the things that make for peace."

Spend time in prayer and journal your thoughts. List any names of those who do not know Jesus as Savior. Then write out a prayer asking Jesus to bring peace to whatever circumstances you are facing.

day five

THE PLOT TO KILL JESUS

"Now the Passover and Unleavened Bread were two days away; and the chief priests and the scribes were seeking how to seize Him by stealth and kill Him; for they were saying, 'Not during the festival, otherwise there might be a riot of the people.'" Mark 14:1-2

It's two days before Passover and the city is crowded with people gathering to commemorate how God freed His people from slavery in Egypt. (*See Exodus Chapter 12*)

Those in authority at the temple were becoming increasingly concerned about how many of their people were choosing to follow Jesus—even proclaiming Him as the Messiah. The Jewish people were indeed looking for a Messiah, one that would establish a government and liberate them from oppressive Roman rule, but this Jesus of Nazareth seemed to be doing nothing but stirring up problems for the priests.

Be open to receiving God's plan for your life

Although the people insisted on proclaiming Him as their King, Jesus did not fit the mold the elite temple authorities expected. And they certainly didn't want the Romans to think they were planning an uprising against Caesar—especially since a large crowd of Jewish people were gathering for the feast.

The priests didn't just want Jesus arrested ensuring they would still have to deal with Him. They wanted Him killed, so they could continue with their religious traditions as it had always been done—all because they were concerned more about their authority and position within society than they were about the One who came to save their souls eternally.

As you stand quietly in the shadow of the cross today, ask yourself what you can learn from the religious authorities. Are you guilty of the same attitude—one where your expectations of what God will do are clouding your discernment and making it impossible for you to see what He is actually doing?

Be open to receiving God's plans for your life, even if those plans don't look like you thought they would. Remember not to risk rejecting the presence of the Lord because you fear what others might think of your beliefs.

Jesus, help me to remember Your Kingdom is the most important. Help me to seek after You and Your plans for my life even when they don't look like I expect. Lord, help me not to be selfish, but to willingly honor You in all I do. In Jesus' name. Amen.

Second Glance: Matthew 26:1-5; Luke 22:1-2; John 11:47-57; Jeremiah 29:1-14

Looking Beyond

We read in today's Scriptures how the chief priests and the scribes were *"seeking how to seize Him by stealth and kill Him."*

We often think of *stealth* to mean: secret, *undetected, not openly acknowledged.* And while this certainly describes how the priests went about their plan, we also see a deeper intent by looking at the Greek word for *stealth—Dolos [dol' os]* which means *deceit, craft(y), with guile (which is sly & cunning in attaining a goal).*

We can see by this that the priests and scribes weren't just plotting for Jesus' arrest in secret, they were acting deceitfully. Behind the scenes, Satan was cunningly asserting his own agenda against God's plans—hoping to kill the Savior of mankind.

And the enemy works the same deceit in our own lives today, hoping we won't notice when he entices us to doubt the purpose God has for our lives, or when we choose to sit quietly by while our beliefs are challenged. Yet, no secret plot can ultimately change the plans of God.

God is in control. And those promises He has made to you are faithful and true. You may feel the enemy has derailed you, but God will use every trial to bring about the purposes He has for your life.

Do you believe this is true? How does it bring you comfort today? Spend time journaling your thoughts and prayers.

day six

JUDAS BETRAYS JESUS

"Then one of the twelve, named Judas Iscariot, went to the chief priests and said, 'What are you willing to give me to betray Him to you?' And they weighed out thirty pieces of silver to him. From then on he began looking for a good opportunity to betray Jesus."
Matthew 26:14-16

Judas is surrounded by money. And it appears he is concerned with material wealth. In John, we see he not only complains about the expensive oil being poured out on to Jesus' feet, but it seems others know he helps himself to the money whenever he likes.

"But Judas Iscariot, one of his disciples (he who was about to betray him), said, 'Why was this ointment not sold for three hundred denarii and given to the poor?' He said this, not because he cared about the poor, but because he was a thief, and having charge of the moneybag he used to help himself to what was put into it." John 12:4-6 ESV

Maybe Judas' desire for money is what drove him to accept the 30 coins of silver in exchange for handing Jesus over to the Pharisees. Maybe he was desperate for a way to pay back the savings he had overused.

Judas is counted among the disciples, yet he struggles with being tempted by money and takes advantage of his entrusted position. It is very possible he had a habit of taking money and then finding ways to replace it. Except this time maybe he's gone too far and he sees accepting the pieces of silver as his only option. How sad, especially considering Jesus would have certainly forgiven the debt that he owed.

Small compromises can have a huge impact

Likewise, we can also become distracted by the material things of this

world. We intend to give our money during offering, but somehow we aren't sure we will have enough for other things. So we withhold just a little—with all intentions of 'making it up' to God with our next offering check.

Little by little we find ourselves taking more and giving less; betraying our commitment to honor God with not just our money, but also our time and skills serving others.

How often do we betray Jesus through our actions by seeking to fulfill our desires rather than pressing in to the calling and purpose He created us for?

But the good news is this: just as Judas' shortcomings didn't disqualify him from being counted among the disciples, neither do our weaknesses keep Jesus from including us in His grace and mercy.

Jesus, forgive me when I seek to fill my life with selfish pursuits rather than seeking relationship with You. Help me to remember my calling from You is more important than anything this world can offer. Thank You, Jesus, that Your grace and mercy are freely given, even when I don't deserve them. In Jesus' name. Amen.

Second Glance: Mark 14:10-11; Luke 22:3-6

Looking Beyond

Today's Scriptures reveal a turning point for Judas. Where he once made a commitment to follow Jesus, he is now making decisions that will change his life.

In Mark 14:10 we see where Judas *"went off to the chief priests."* The Greek word for *went off* is *Aperchomai [ap-erkh'-om-ahee]* which means *go away, depart.*

One of its root words is the same as we saw on Day One—*Apo [apo']* which means *separation.* The other root word is *Erchomai [er-khom-ahee]* which means *to come from one place to another.*

Whether Judas made a conscious decision to turn from following Christ or not, I can't say for certain. However, we can see by the original context there was definitely a change in Judas' path. He changes direction and departs from one place to come to another place.

Just like Judas, we must be careful we don't allow our decisions to cause us to follow the wrong path. You may not think a small, simple choice could lead you away from Jesus, but even one small compromise can have a huge impact.

When they were younger, I would often tell my kids, "It's a slippery slope when you make the wrong choices, but it's not always a steep one." Meaning one little step might not sink you to the bottom, but each day you inch a little further away from where you started.

You made a good decision on Day One of this journey to give up anything that would distract from following Jesus. Why not take a few minutes today to review the list you wrote. Ask God to help you revise the items on your list. Do you need to add something?

Are there any things you have noticed as particularly tempting for you? Do you find yourself struggling to balance everyday demands with following after Jesus? Write those struggles down.

Spend time in prayer asking God to help you continue following after Him.

day seven

PASSOVER PREPARATION

"Then came the first day of Unleavened Bread on which the Passover lamb had to be sacrificed. And Jesus sent Peter and John, saying, 'Go and prepare the Passover for us, so that we may eat it.' They said to Him, 'Where do You want us to prepare it?' And He said to them, 'When you have entered the city, a man will meet you carrying a pitcher of water; follow him into the house that he enters. And you shall say to the owner of the house, "The Teacher says to you, 'Where is the guest room in which I may eat the Passover with My disciples?'" 'And he will show you a large, furnished upper room; prepare it there.' And they left and found everything just as He had told them; and they prepared the Passover." Luke 22:7-13

As the Passover approaches, the disciples make preparations for Jesus and His followers to observe the traditional, Jewish festival commemorating the Israelites' freedom from Egypt.

At first reading, it would be easy for us to discuss Peter and John's immediate obedience in following Christ's instructions to them. However, I'd like to look at this from someone else's perspective—the master of the house.

In reading these Scriptures, notice the man had a space already furnished and ready for use. Initially, I wondered if he had such a close relationship with God that he was obedient to the prompting to make this room available for something more.

> **Jesus, help me make room for MORE of You in my daily routine**

These verses don't seem to reveal *why* this area has been prepared for use. But as you'll see in the *Looking Beyond* section, there was indeed a reason there was room for the Messiah.

One thing is certain, God looked down from Heaven and saw the willingness of this man to make available all his earthly possessions to be used in whatever way his Provider willed.

And because he made room—room for more—he was granted the privilege of the Messiah's presence, the Savior of his soul sat in the place where he made room.

Have you made room for more in your daily schedule? More of Him? More of His blessing? More of His Word? More of whatever He asks of you?

Lord, I want to make more room for You. I want to open up the spaces I have kept for myself and allow You to come and spend time with me. Jesus, help me prepare room for You in my daily routine. Help me to clean out the cobwebs of chaos and allow Your presence to fill me with more. In Jesus' name. Amen.

Second Glance: Matthew 26:17-19; Mark 14:12-16

Looking Beyond

As I mentioned earlier, when I first read these verses I didn't know why the owner of the home had a room fully furnished and ready to receive guests.

A quick glance at the Greek word *Kataluma [kat-al'-oo-mah]* reveals the meaning of *room* as *a lodging place or inn*. This is the same word used in Luke 2:7.

"And she gave birth to her firstborn son; and she wrapped Him in cloths, and laid Him in a manger, because there was no room for them in the inn." Luke 2:7

In the days right before His birth, there was no room for Jesus. He even spent His entire ministry with no real place to rest His head and call home (Luke 9:58).

And now we find, here in the His last days, room is made for Jesus. All because one man offered up his unused space for Jesus to prepare of the Passover, and ultimately the cross.

As we take this next step in Jesus' journey toward the cross, He spends quality time with those He loves most, preparing their hearts for what lies ahead. I invite you to imagine yourself as the innkeeper. Your own home is host to the Messiah and you can hear the words He speaks as He washes the disciples' feet, breaks bread, and shares His heart with His friends.

Have you made room for Jesus? Do you offer your heart, your home, your time as a place for Jesus to come, sit, and dwell? Is there more you can offer?

Journal your thoughts and prayers on how you can make room for more.

day eight

JESUS WASHES THE DISCIPLES' FEET

"Now before the Feast of the Passover, Jesus knowing that His hour had come that He would depart out of this world to the Father, having loved His own who were in the world, He loved them to the end...Then He poured water into the basin, and began to wash the disciples' feet and to wipe them with the towel with which He was girded...So when He had washed their feet, and taken His garments and reclined at the table again, He said to them, 'Do you know what I have done to you?'" John 13:1,5,12

During the Passover supper, as Jesus sat around the table looking at each disciple, one by one, He knew all the ways in which they would soon fail Him—betrayal, denial, abandonment.

He rose from the table, removed His outer garment, wrapped Himself in the pureness of a clean towel and began to wash away their filth. A foretelling of the events soon to come.

Jesus shows us how to love through the hurt and never give up

He loved them to the end.

As He knelt at the feet of Judas, staring up into his eyes, He knew of the betrayal that was planned, and yet He did not withhold His love.

Bowing before Peter, He probably smiled slightly, because He knew Peter was passionate and eager. But He also knew he would deny Him three times. Yet, He pressed in all the more; He loved him to the end.

He humbled Himself in front of each one of these men knowing they would scatter and abandon Him during His last hours. He bowed

Himself low, took on the role of a servant, and loved them to the end.

As the hours ahead placed a heavy weight on Jesus' heart, He knew it would also bring sorrow for the disciples. Still He never pulled away to protect His own heart or to make it easier for the ones He loved.

Jesus clothed Himself in sacrifice, bowed Himself low, and wiped clean the filthiest part of all of us—our soul.

He withheld nothing. He loved us to the end.

> **"Greater love has no one than this,**
> **that one lay down his life for his friends."**
> John 15:13

Jesus, there are so many times I don't feel deserving of Your love. Thank You for loving me no matter how many times I fail. Your willingness to go to the cross knowing I will mess up anyway is humbling and amazing. Thank You for loving me so tenderly and unconditionally. Help me to press into relationships when things get tough. Help me to be an example of You to others. In Jesus' name. Amen.

Second Glance: John 13:1-17

Looking Beyond

"So when He had washed their feet, and taken His garments and reclined at the table again, He said to them, 'Do you know what I have done to you?...For I gave you an example that you also should do as I did to you.'" John 13:12, 15

In today's Scripture verses, Jesus gives the disciples a visual example of what He is preparing to do spiritually on the cross. As He takes off His outer garment, places a servant's apron around His waist and begins to wash their dirty feet, He is sending the message that He is taking upon Himself humanity and all of the filthy sin that comes with it.

Likewise, when He is finished, He resumes His rightful place at the table symbolizing that once His sacrifice is finished on the cross, He will resume His place at the right hand of God.

"...but He, having offered one sacrifice for sins for all time, sat down at the right hand of God." Hebrews 10:12

Yet, it is not just the message of the cross He conveys in this display of unconditional love. In one beautiful moment Jesus shows us how to press in, to love through the hurt, and never give up.

He knew they were going to betray Him and He could have so easily pulled away to protect His own heart, but He loved them through it.

And even though the disciples didn't understand everything happening, much less the symbolism of it all, they allowed themselves to be loved. What an important lesson for us, too.

When we find ourselves struggling through hard relationships, we often pull away to protect our hearts—not giving nor receiving love. But the disciples get it right, despite their confusion and uncertainty, they accept Jesus' act of unconditional love.

Let's take a few minutes to evaluate our love toward others.

It doesn't take long in any relationship, with either friend or family member, before we encounter disagreements and disappointments.

When we find ourselves facing a relationship challenge:

- Do we press in past the hard?
- Do we make an effort to serve the other person, even if we don't feel like they have earned it?
- Do we love them to the end?
- Do we allow others to love us to the end?
- Do we make room for love?
- Or, do we scatter attempting to protect our own hearts in the discomfort of disagreement?

Take time today to meditate on these questions, write down your thoughts. Also, tell the ones you care about that you love them, especially those who have wronged you in some way.

UNCHANGED BY JESUS

"Now when evening came, Jesus was reclining at the table with the twelve disciples. As they were eating, He said, 'Truly I say to you that one of you will betray Me.' Being deeply grieved, they each one began to say to Him, 'Surely not I, Lord?' And He answered, 'He who dipped his hand with Me in the bowl is the one who will betray Me. The Son of Man is to go, just as it is written of Him; but woe to that man by whom the Son of Man is betrayed! It would have been good for that man if he had not been born.' And Judas, who was betraying Him, said, 'Surely it is not I, Rabbi?' Jesus said to him, 'You have said it yourself.'" Matthew 26:20-25

Jesus has just finished washing the disciples' feet, an intimate moment He shared with each man, when He reveals one of them will betray Him. Their reaction was deep sorrow.

They were a close group of friends, spending all their time together. How could this even be a possibility? Who would dare betray Him? Maybe it wasn't someone else, maybe it was them. Each one began to question if they were capable of betraying their Friend—even Judas.

How strange he would ask the question considering he had already accepted a deal for 30 pieces of silver in exchange for his Teacher. But Judas hid his true intentions so well even the disciples did not suspect him as the betrayer.

From the outside, Judas' daily life looked just like that of a follower of Jesus. He walked, talked, and acted like a disciple, but inside Judas continued to struggle with money-issues and bad decisions. It appears he never allowed his time with Jesus to bring real change to his life or his heart.

Scripture doesn't indicate that Judas was moved in any way when Jesus revealed His knowledge of the disciple's plan to betray Him. But, in John chapter 13, we see Satan was allowed to enter Judas and Jesus dismisses him to go carry out his intended plan.

"After the morsel, Satan then entered into him. Therefore Jesus said to him, 'What you do, do quickly.'... So after receiving the morsel he went out immediately; and it was night."
John 13:27, 30

Although Jesus knew God's plan for Him to go to the cross would be carried out one way or another, how heartbreaking it must have been for Him to watch as Satan entered His friend and took over the plans set in motion by Judas.

Jesus loves you —even when you stumble

Judas was with Jesus every day and had every opportunity to make changes to his life, yet he chose to remain untouched by the presence of God in his life.

As you sit in the shadows of the upper room watching Jesus talk with the disciples, you can also ask yourself:

- Am I allowing my time with Jesus to change me?
- Have I, like Judas, spent time wearing a mask and pretending I am okay when I'm not?
- Have I turned away from Jesus to pursue my own plans without concern of what He thinks?

Lord, I don't want to pretend anymore. I want You to bring real change in my life. Help me to be open to Your Words and the plans You have for me. Show me how to make small changes everyday that will help me to become more like the person You created me to be. In Jesus' name. Amen.

Second Glance: Mark 14:17-21; Luke 22:21-23; John 13:18-30

Looking Beyond

During the Passover meal, the exchange between Jesus and the disciples finds Jesus revealing He will be betrayed. In John 13, Peter prompts John to ask Jesus who it is that will betray Him.

Jesus replies, *"That is the one for whom I shall dip the morsel and give it to him."* (vs.26) Once Jesus dips the morsel, He gives it to Judas.

Of note, the Greek word for *dip* is *Bapto [bap'-to]* which means *to dip in*. But there is a footnote which said it shouldn't be confused with the Greek word *Baptizo [bap-tid'-zo]* which means *to dip repeatedly, to immerse; to clean by submerging.*

The picture this paints is one of dunking rather than immersing something and allowing it to penetrate. For example, think of a cream-stuffed cookie. Some like to dip it into milk. It coats the outside, but the cookie remains crunchy and relatively unchanged. Others like to immerse the cookie in the milk, leaving it to become soft and saturated with the milk.

This is a great illustration of what happened in the life of Judas. He was surrounded by Jesus and His teachings, but he didn't allow himself to become completely submerged, saturated, or changed.

If we aren't careful, we can do the same. We can read our Bibles, blogs and social media posts, and attend Bible study, but never really allow the person of Jesus to make a change in our lives.

Today, spend some time reading the account of Jesus' exchange with His disciples about His betrayer. Imagine you are in the room listening to His words. Ask yourself the questions listed above. Journal your thoughts and prayers.

day ten

PASSOVER

"And when He had taken some bread and given thanks, He broke it and gave it to them, saying, 'This is My body which is given for you; do this in remembrance of Me.' And in the same way He took the cup after they had eaten, saying, 'This cup which is poured out for you is the new covenant in My blood.'" Luke 22:19-20

This intimate dinner among brothers was full of history and tradition, but it also symbolized the soon coming sacrifice of the Teacher and Friend they had grown to cherish.

The Jewish people had been commemorating the Passover for hundreds of years. Remembering when they were enslaved in Egypt and the presence of the blood of a sacrificed lamb over the doorposts was the sign for death to pass over the homes of the Israelites. *(For a history of the first Passover read Exodus 12 and see Looking Beyond below.)*

God's gift of eternal life is for everyone

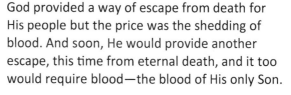

God provided a way of escape from death for His people but the price was the shedding of blood. And soon, He would provide another escape, this time from eternal death, and it too would require blood—the blood of His only Son.

As Jesus breaks the unleavened bread of the Passover meal, it signifies His body that will be bruised and torn during the crucifixion process.

He then distributes the bread to each of them. Another symbolic gesture—the giving of His body for each person. His gift of eternal life is for everyone. Every. One.

Then Christ blesses one of the four cups of wine during a Passover meal (some believe it was the third cup of the meal which symbolized redemption and blessing), and He proclaims the new covenant—the forgiveness and restoration through the spilling of His blood, our sacrificial Lamb.

Jesus tells the disciples, *"do this in remembrance of me."* This meal had always commemorated the passing over of death from their ancestors' homes, but now Jesus wants them (and us) to also remember His death and resurrection as the ultimate passing over of death.

Can you see how God weaves together what He did for the Israelites with what He did at the cross for us? Today, take a few moments to read about the Passover and say a prayer of thanks for His sacrificial love.

Maybe gather some juice or wine and crackers or bread and take a few moments alone with Jesus to remember what He did for you on the cross as you read Matthew 26:26-28.

Father, Thank You for loving me enough to send Your only Son as the sacrifice needed for my sin. Jesus, Thank You for Your obedience to the Father in giving Your life for me. Lord, there are no words to express my awe or how humbled I feel to be Your child. Thank You Jesus for Your love. In Jesus' name. Amen.

Second Glance: Matthew 26:26-29; Mark 14:22-25; Luke 22:14-20

Looking Beyond

Let's look at a little bit of the history of the first Passover, which you can read about in Exodus chapters 7-12.

When the Israelites were enslaved in Egypt, God sent Moses and Aaron to Pharaoh to request the release of His people. Pharaoh refused and what happened next was of epic proportion—literally.

God warned Moses that Pharaoh's heart would be hardened and the Israelites would only be allowed to leave when God had brought *"great acts of judgement"* (Exodus 7:4) against the Egyptians for their harsh treatment against His people.

God brought 10 plagues against the Egyptians and each time Pharaoh's anger increased towards Moses and the Israelites, until the final plague which caused Pharaoh to essentially throw them out of Egypt.

The final plague? Death. God told Moses the Lord would go out into the town after midnight and cause death to fall on every firstborn—both human and animal.

However, He instructed Moses that each Israelite family should sacrifice a lamb, take the blood and apply it to the doorposts and across the top of the door support. When the Lord saw the blood applied to the door, He would pass over that home and not cause death to the family. He also gave them specific instructions on how to prepare the lamb for their supper and what to eat with the meal. They were to eat with their clothes and shoes on, staff in hand, ready to leave in haste.

The bread was to be made without any leaven, or yeast, which they would eat in the desert as they fled from Egypt.

The bread is known as the *"bread of affliction"* (Deuteronomy 16:3) and was a foretelling of Jesus' comments at the last supper with His disciples when He tells them the bread is His *"body given for you."* He was making the connection that His body would be afflicted for them...and us.

We already discussed a few similarities between the first Passover and the meal Jesus shared with His friends. Read the Passover Scriptures below and then write any other similarities you find.

Second Glance at the Passover:
Exodus 12; Deuteronomy 16:1-8; Leviticus 23:4-8; Numbers 28:16-25

JESUS PREDICTS PETER'S DENIAL

"After singing a hymn, they went out to the Mount of Olives. And Jesus said to them, 'You will all fall away, because it is written, "I will strike down the shepherd, and the sheep shall be scattered." But after I have been raised, I will go ahead of you to Galilee.' But Peter said to Him, 'Even though all may fall away, yet I will not.' And Jesus said to him, 'Truly I say to you, that this very night, before a rooster crows twice, you yourself will deny Me three times.' But Peter kept saying insistently, 'Even if I have to die with You, I will not deny You!' And they all were saying the same thing also." Mark 14:26-31

Simon Peter—so in love with Jesus; so sure of his faith—declares he would follow Jesus to the end, even so far as to embrace death for his Friend, the One he knows is the Son of God.

And yet Jesus sees inside his heart, He sees where Peter will compromise, unknowingly fulfilling the warning of Jesus. He tells Peter the truth, "You will deny me three times."

I can only imagine what Peter must have felt when he heard Jesus speak those words. Something inside of him must have known it was true because they were the words spoken by the One who calls Heaven home, and yet he was so sure, positive that his faithfulness to Christ was real.

I imagine Peter wondered:
"How could it be that Jesus sees denial in me? How could rejection even be a possibility? Haven't people seen me with Him? Doesn't everyone know I am close to Him? Don't they see the change in my life because of Him? How could I possibly deny being part of Christ?"

No matter what trials you face, they do not take God by surprise

As you journey closer to the cross, the world will demand a response —do you know Jesus? Have you spent time with Him? Are you the same? Or, have you been changed?

Jesus, help me to remain faithful when life gets tough and presses in on all sides. Help me to show Your love, grace, and mercy during the hard times. May my life be a witness of who You are and how You have made all the difference in me. Lord, help me to stand firm in my faith; help me to show You through my actions and interactions with others. In Jesus' name. Amen.

Second Glance: Matthew 26:31-35; Luke 22:31-34; John 13:36-38

Looking Beyond

"Simon, Simon, behold, Satan has demanded permission to sift you like wheat; but I have prayed for you, that your faith may not fail; and you, when once you have turned again, strengthen your brothers." Luke 22:31-32

Peter has just experienced some incredible moments—the Passover meal, Judas leaving in the middle of dinner, Jesus washing everyone's feet—and all of sudden Jesus looks over and tells him Satan has demanded to test his faith.

Wow. That must have felt like a gut-punch that takes the breath right out of you. I can't imagine how Peter must have felt in that moment. But Jesus tells him two important things. And He means for us to cling to them, also.

First, Jesus says, *"I have prayed for you."* What better person could you have praying for you when you are going through a test of faith? Jesus knew this was going to be one of the hardest times for Peter and His immediate reaction was to pray for His friend. The Greek for *pray* is *Deomai [deh'-om-ahee], ask; beg*. Jesus begged the Father that Peter's faith would not fail during this testing.

Second, Jesus encourages Peter there will be an end to the testing and when it's over, God will use it to help Peter *"strengthen [his] brothers."*

This is the same message Jesus has for you. No matter what trials you face, they do not take God by surprise. He knew you would face testing of your faith. And once you come out on the other side, you should use your experience to encourage others, build them up, point them to the One who saw you through.

Are you going through a faith test right now? As you stand in the shadow of the cross, looking up to where your Savior will hang, will you stand firm in your faith? Will you declare Him as your Lord?

Will others see Jesus in the way you live your life?

Spend time reading through today's key Scripture passage. Consider copying it into your journal and reading it out loud. As you read, think about the questions above. Imagine you are looking up at the cross, ask God to speak to your heart and give you strength and boldness to withstand the testing of your faith.

In The Shadow Of The Cross

JESUS PRAYS IN THE GARDEN

"And He came out and proceeded as was His custom to the Mount of Olives; and the disciples also followed Him. When He arrived at the place, He said to them, 'Pray that you may not enter into temptation.' And He withdrew from them about a stone's throw, and He knelt down and began to pray, saying, 'Father, if You are willing, remove this cup from Me; yet not My will, but Yours be done.' Now an angel from heaven appeared to Him, strengthening Him. And being in agony He was praying very fervently; and His sweat became like drops of blood, falling down upon the ground. When He rose from prayer, He came to the disciples and found them sleeping from sorrow, and said to them, 'Why are you sleeping? Get up and pray that you may not enter into temptation.'" Luke 22:39-46

Jesus, full of sorrow, seeks to be in the presence of His Father. He falls on His face and cries from the depths of His spirit. While the impending circumstances were different than ever before, this particular scenario was familiar.

Jesus regularly sought time alone with the Father in this special place on the Mount of Olives—*"as was His custom."* This wasn't a one time occurrence for when times were exceptionally tough. This was the way Jesus renewed His spirit, refreshed Himself after giving so much in ministry, and where He met with God in true relationship.

Jesus sees your burden-weary heart

On this particular evening, Jesus doesn't pray once and give up. He continues going back to talk to His Father. He presses in harder, cries out more—even to the point of great stress and agony. And yet God doesn't fail to meet Him there. He sees His Son, hears His cries and sends an angel to minister to Him as He agonizes and darkness closes in around Him.

Even as He seeks God in distress He asks one thing from His disciples—wait and pray.

He asks the same of us today. Whether we find ourselves facing difficult, heart-heavy circumstances or just in need of daily direction from God, we should seek a quiet place of retreat and pray—then wait on Him to speak. He sees our burden-weary hearts and He hears our cries. And He will answer us according to His will and His timing.

What are some ways you can dedicate time for prayer and waiting for His voice daily?

Jesus, help me to remember to make time for You during my day. I pray You will meet me in my difficult times and speak Your will to my heart. Help me to hear Your voice and follow Your plan for my life. In Jesus' name. Amen.

Second Glance: Matthew 26:36-46; Mark 14:32-42

Looking Beyond

Just before going to the garden to pray, Jesus told Peter Satan had asked to test him and that Peter will, in fact, deny Jesus. Peter is adamant he will follow Jesus anywhere—even to death. Yet here we see Peter struggle to simply stay awake and help Jesus pray.

Jesus comes to Peter and warns him, *"Keep watching and praying that you may not enter into temptation; the spirit is willing, but the flesh is weak."* (Matthew 26:41)

The Greek word for *watch* is *Gregoreuo [gray-gor-yoo'-o]* which means *give strict attention, to take heed lest through remission and indolence destructive calamity suddenly overtakes one.* What this means is that Jesus is telling Peter, "I know your spirit is willing to brave these trials but your flesh is weak. You need to pay attention and pray because if you're lazy in this, destruction will suddenly overtake you."

That's a pretty stern warning. Not just for Peter, but also for us. If we are not willing to do the hard work and pray and be watchful when trials and temptations come, we will find ourselves being overtaken.

The good news is Jesus tells us the way to endure—watch and pray. We should pay attention when we feel like we are being tempted to take a different path than the one God would have us take. Pray for His direction.

Remember what we read yesterday in *Looking Beyond: "No matter what trial you are going through, it didn't take God by surprise. He knew you would face a testing of your faith. And once you come out on the other side, you should use it to encourage others."*

Think about a time when you struggled through a difficult circumstance. Write down how God ministered to you then. Were there specific verses or prayers that helped and comforted you?

Write those down. Pray for God to show you how you can encourage someone else this week using what He taught you in that trial.

Maybe, just as Jesus asked three of His closest friends to pray with Him, you could invite someone to pray with and for you regularly.

THE ARREST OF JESUS

"While He was still speaking, behold, Judas, one of the twelve, came up accompanied by a large crowd with swords and clubs, who came from the chief priests and elders of the people. Now he who was be-traying Him gave them a sign, saying, 'Whomever I kiss, He is the one; seize Him.' Immediately Judas went to Jesus and said, 'Hail, Rabbi!' and kissed Him. And Jesus said to him, 'Friend, do what you have come for.' Then they came and laid hands on Jesus and seized Him... At that time Jesus said to the crowds, 'Have you come out with swords and clubs to arrest Me as you would against a robber? Every day I used to sit in the temple teaching and you did not seize Me.'"
Matthew 26:47-50, 55

As Jesus completes His time of prayer in the garden with the Father, He immediately looks up to see Judas approaching.

The time has come.

Trust Jesus with the place in your heart that needs healing

The shadow of the cross grows darker as Jesus now faces the beginning of a series of events that will leave Him heartbroken and crying out to the Father.

As these moments unfold, Jesus remains com-posed and true to His divine character, even with the knowledge of what was to come next.

He speaks gently, but honestly, to Judas. He remains in control of the situation when the servant's ear is cut off. And He still bestows heal-ing to the one who has come to seize Him.

In all the chaos of the night, Jesus speaks a hard truth to the priests:

"I was in your presence and yet you never laid hands on me."

While the intended meaning is that they had every opportunity to arrest Him publicly yet chose to do so in the darkness and secret of night, another way we can look at Jesus' words is this: He is in our midst day after day and we never grab on to Him.

Too often we fail to take time to reach out and seize His presence in our daily struggles, even though He is there and waiting—in control, speaking gentle truth, acting with kindness, and ready to give us whatever we need.

Just as Jesus approached the cross and the shadow grew darker, at times it can seem like despite growing closer to Jesus, we may still find ourselves in hard, often heartbreaking, situations.

Just like He remained in control in the garden, He is in control in your situation, too. Are you willing to follow Jesus through dark times, as He guides you through the shadows?

Lord, I thank You for Your steady presence in times of gut-wrenching heartache. Without You I wouldn't know how to navigate the dark valleys. Jesus, help me to reach out to You, hold tight to Your presence, and allow You to lead me through life's trials and temptations. In Jesus' name. Amen.

Second Glance: Matthew 26:47-56; Mark 14:43-50; Luke 22:47-53

Looking Beyond

Jesus' response to those who came to seize Him in the garden is important for us to consider, but let's not overlook how He responds to His betrayer, Judas.

Judas greets Jesus with a term of honor—*Rabbi [Rhabbi] (hrab-bee')* which is a title used when a Jewish student addresses their teacher. Judas then completes his greeting with a kiss. There are three different words used in the Scriptures for this one kiss.

First, Judas tells the priests and scribes he will signal who Jesus is by a kiss: *Phileo [fil-eh'-o] – which means to befriend, some affection, great kindly.*

Then Scripture says once Judas greets Jesus with a term of honor, he gives him a kiss: *Kataphileo [kat-af-ee-leh'-o] – which means to kiss much, kiss again and again, kiss tenderly.*

In Luke 22:47-53, Jesus responds to Judas by asking if he has come to betray Him with a kiss: *Philema [fil'-ay-mah] – which was the custom of greeting one another.*

So, in effect, Judas says to the chief priests and elders seeking Jesus, "Hey guys, I'm going to give you a sign and it's going to be the person whom I show kindness toward by giving them a kiss." His actions convey an outward show of kindness, yet the motive of his heart is not pure.

When Judas is actually facing Jesus, he kisses Him tenderly. He pretends to connect with his Teacher; he pretends to show his affection toward Him.

But Jesus says, "No, no, no, Judas. This isn't love. This is just a routine custom you are performing toward me. This is just an empty kiss—where is your heart?"

How many times have we approached Jesus in worship with the same attitude—one that is an outward show of kindness toward Jesus but our hearts are not right?

We pretend to give our affection to the Father, but in reality we are just going through the motions, carrying out a routine we are accustomed to, our hearts never connecting in true relationship with our Savior. Jesus wants so much more from us. He deserves so much more from us.

As you walk a little closer to Jesus' final moments, will you allow Christ to mend the tender places in your heart so you can give Him your true affection?

Spend time asking Jesus to show you the places in your heart that need healing. Pray for Him to make you aware of times you fail to connect with Him in worship or speak empty words instead of honest praise. Journal your thoughts and prayers.

day fourteen

THE JEWISH TRIAL OF JESUS

"...But later on two came forward, and said, 'This man stated, I am able to destroy the temple of God and to rebuild it in three days.' The high priest stood up and said to Him, 'Do You not answer? What is it that these men are testifying against You?' But Jesus kept silent. And the high priest said to Him, 'I adjure You by the living God, that You tell us whether You are the Christ, the Son of God.' Jesus said to him, 'You have said it yourself; nevertheless I tell you, hereafter you will see the Son of Man sitting at the right hand of power, and coming on the clouds of heaven.' Then the high priest tore his robes and said, 'He has blasphemed! What further need do we have of witnesses? Behold, you have now heard the blasphemy; what do you think?' They answered, 'He deserves death!' Then they spat in His face and beat Him with their fists; and others slapped Him, and said, 'Prophesy to us, You Christ; who is the one who hit You?'" Matthew 26:60-68

After soldiers seized Jesus, they brought Him before the high priest as the crowd cast accusations and false testimony at Him.

You are never alone

Jesus walks the shadows with you

Over and over again Jesus was questioned and pressed to give an answer to the reports being given. And He remained silent. No words. No arguments. No objections.

There was no need for Him to explain Himself. He was blameless, sinless, and without fault.

No answer was required; His life was the only evidence required to prove His character. Besides, Jesus knew they were intent on having Him killed, and no matter what answer He gave, they would pile on more false testimony to satisfy His sentence.

Jesus allowed the events to unfold the way Heaven intended. He didn't get in the way of the process. He didn't try to change the direction of the events. He just silently allowed them to happen.

From this moment forward, Jesus says very little. He goes through the process of trials, sentencing, and punishment with few words. He has poured out His heart in anguish to His Father the night before, but now He will fulfill His purpose. Jesus faces the darkest hours ahead without His friends, only the Father to offer strength and comfort.

As we follow after Jesus, we may face criticism and accusations, too, but we are never alone. We have Jesus, walking through the shadows with us...because He's already been there. And we can confidently face the plans God has for us, allowing them to unfold, without trying to change the outcome.

Lord, help me to follow Your example when I find myself being criticized or tested. Give me the strength to remain silent and let my actions be the witness of Your presence in my life. I trust You to be the answer in these trying times. Give me courage in the face of uncertainty, allowing Your plans and purposes for me to unfold. In Jesus' name. Amen.

Second Glance: Matthew 26:57-68; Mark 14:53-65; Luke 22:66-71; John 18:19-24

Looking Beyond

The law of Moses states in Leviticus that anyone found guilty of showing contempt or lack of reverence for God or claiming to have the attributes of God, which is known as blasphemy, was to be put to death by stoning.

"'Moreover, the one who blasphemes the name of the LORD shall surely be put to death; all the congregation shall certainly stone him. The alien as well as the native, when he blasphemes the Name, shall be put to death.'" Leviticus 24:16

The Jewish priests and elders concluded Jesus was guilty of blasphemy and deserved death, however they could not order Him to that punishment because Roman law forbid them from condemning someone to death (John 18:31). In order to have Jesus put to death, the priests needed the Roman Governor to pronounce the sentence.

Therefore, after Jesus had been questioned by the priests and elders, He was taken to the Governor, Pilate, so he could hand down a death sentence. *(We will learn more about the complicated political system between the Jewish rulers and the Roman government later.)*

Did you notice how Mosaic Law required stoning for blasphemy? But remember, Jesus had foreshadowed His crucifixion in previous conversations with His followers about taking up their own crosses. This tells us He already knew the Romans would convict and punish Him to death in their own fashion. Jesus always knew He would be handed over to the Romans for crucifixion.

Imagine yourself standing among the crowd as Jesus was dragged to Pilate's palace by the religious leaders, so blinded by their traditions and customs they believed He was a liar and a fraud.

Ask yourself these challenging questions:

- Do I do the things I do and believe the things I believe because it's just the way it's always been or because God's Word has shaped my thoughts and actions?
- Am I so wrapped up in Christian traditions and expectations that I would miss the Messiah if He walked in to my church?
- Am I quick to jump to conclusions about someone's faith if they don't fit in with my notions of how a Christian should look or act or talk?

Journal your thoughts as you pray and ask God to reveal the places inside where you need to be more open to Him.

day fifteen

PETER DENIES JESUS

"After they had kindled a fire in the middle of the courtyard and had sat down together, Peter was sitting among them. And a servant-girl, seeing him as he sat in the firelight and looking intently at him, said, 'This man was with Him too.' But he denied it, saying, 'Woman, I do not know Him.' A little later, another saw him and said, 'You are one of them too!' But Peter said, 'Man, I am not!' After about an hour had passed, another man began to insist, saying, 'Certainly this man also was with Him, for he is a Galilean too.' But Peter said, 'Man, I do not know what you are talking about.' Immediately, while he was still speaking, a rooster crowed. The Lord turned and looked at Peter. And Peter remembered the word of the Lord, how He had told him, 'Before a rooster crows today, you will deny Me three times.' And he went out and wept bitterly." Luke 22:55-62

Just a few hours earlier, when Jesus predicted his denial, Peter insisted he would never betray his Friend. Simon Peter is adamant he would proclaim his loyalty at all costs, even unto death.

As he sits warming himself by a fire inside the high priest's courtyard after Jesus has been arrested, Peter is questioned about his relationship with the Teacher. And without hesitation, in a moment of self-preservation, Peter denies knowing Jesus.

Don't allow fear to choke out faith

And again, twice more they ask if he is associated with Jesus, and each time as fear grips Peter he denies his deep relationship with Christ. As the final denial passes Peter's lips a rooster crows and Jesus lifts His eyes to find Peter's, piercing his soul with deep anguish as the truth of the words of the Master echoes in his heart, *"you will deny Me."*

Peter was so sure he wasn't that person—one to deny his deep love for his Friend. And yet here he stood, looking into the eyes of the One he loved, having denied Him. It was more than Peter could bear and he ran away and wept bitterly.

In those brief moments of denial Peter didn't calculate his answer, he didn't plan to deny Christ, he simply feared what would happen if he professed his relationship with Jesus.

Like Peter, we don't intend to deny Christ in our lives. We profess our love for God and our relationship with Christ, but how often do we deny His sovereignty over our situations by allowing fear to choke out faith?

There may come a day when your faith is tested by death—whether because of illness, accident, or even threat of violence. Will you willingly face down the threat and proclaim your love for Jesus?

Jesus, help me to be faithful to You as You have been faithful to me. Give me the strength to proclaim Your name even when it isn't popular, comfortable, or acceptable. Help me not to fear my circumstances, but to trust in Your ability to handle every situation. Give me the boldness to know You will protect me and keep me close to You. In Jesus' name. Amen.

Second Glance: Matthew 26:69-75; Mark 14:66-72; John 18:15-18; 25-27

Looking Beyond

It's been a very long day for our group of friends. Peter is tired, as evidenced by his falling asleep in the garden while Jesus prayed. He's cold and just wants to warm himself by the fire and observe what happens to his Friend.

Jesus had cautioned him, *"Keep watching and praying that you may not enter into temptation; the spirit is willing, but the flesh is weak."* (Matthew 26:41)

This is the moment Jesus warned him about and yet, he didn't recognize it. He didn't discern this is a testing of his faith in the face of fear. He just said what he needed to say to remain hidden and survive the night.

When Peter realizes what has happened and finds Jesus looking into his eyes, it's more than he can bear. Peter was in absolute agony over what he had done. I imagine he may have even gone back to the same garden where Jesus had prayed, and wailed a soul-wrenching cry.

This is the same type of weeping we read about on Day Four when Jesus wept—*Klaio [klah'-yo]*, which means *to mourn, or weep as the sign of pain and grief, mourn for, and bewail (great bitterness).*

Peter was in full repentance over his failure. He wasn't just sorry he did it, he truly was grieved in his spirit and perhaps allowed himself to remember Jesus' promise, *"...and you, when once you have turned again, strengthen your brothers."* (Luke 22:32)

Jesus has already acknowledged there would be restoration and forgiveness for Peter. And his experience would give him the ability to strengthen others. Peter sought God for his restoration and forgiveness, such a contrast to Judas' response to his own short-comings.

"Then when Judas, who had betrayed Him, saw that He had been condemned, he felt remorse and returned the thirty pieces of silver to the chief priests and elders, saying, 'I have sinned by betraying innocent blood.' ...And he threw the pieces of silver into the temple sanctuary and departed; and he went away and hanged himself."
Matthew 27:3-4a, 5

Judas may have been sorry for what he had done because he didn't intend the severity of the outcome for Jesus, but he tried to remedy the situation himself. He didn't seek repentance and forgiveness from God, but tried to make it right in his own power.

How often do we do the same? When we find ourselves in a messed up situation we may have even created, our response must be to seek out God and His forgiveness rather than trying to control the situation.

As we walk alongside Jesus, remember the purpose of His journey to the cross is forgiveness and restoration with God. As Christians, we don't often like to dwell on our shortcomings, but the reality is we still sin. We won't be made perfect until we arrive in Heaven. Each day we deny or betray Jesus in some way.

Today's assignment may be difficult, but spend time in prayer asking God to show you unconfessed sin in your life. Then, ask God for forgiveness and for the compassion to use your experiences to help others. If you need to, write out your prayer.

Read more about Peter's restoration: John 21:1-17

THE ROMAN TRIAL OF JESUS

"Now Jesus stood before the governor, and the governor questioned Him, saying, 'Are You the King of the Jews?' And Jesus said to him, 'It is as you say.' And while He was being accused by the chief priests and elders, He did not answer. Then Pilate said to Him, 'Do You not hear how many things they testify against You?' And He did not answer him with regard to even a single charge, so the governor was quite amazed." Matthew 27:11-14

"Are you the King of the Jews?" One question seeking to sum up Jesus' identity and purpose.

"It is as you say." Jesus directs this one answer back at the inquirer.

As the shadow of the cross darkens, we are asked the same question, "Is Jesus King?" What will we answer?

> **Forgiveness is the ultimate goal of the cross**

Sometimes when we ask Him into our lives we still don't allow Him full control. We hold tight to the dreams we want to manage, the sin we excuse as a bad habit, or the pain we've allowed to shape our identity.

When we refuse to grant Him access to the deep places in our hearts where unforgiveness and bitterness take root we, too, strip Him of His rightful reign. To give Him full authority, we must give up our self-appointed right to be offended, even when we have experienced wrong done to us.

In the next hours before the cross, Jesus will be mistreated and abused in unthinkable ways, yet He presses onward. He willingly takes the punishment for the sins of the whole world, so that His

Father could forgive us and we could forgive each other. Forgiveness is the ultimate goal of the cross. He doesn't allow the wrong done to Him by others to deter Him from His purpose. He forgives the very ones inflicting pain.

"But Jesus was saying, 'Father, forgive them; for they do not know what they are doing.'" Luke 23:34

As He draws closer to the cross, will you allow yourself to draw closer to Him? As you imagine the abuse He prepares to endure, are you willing to carry your deepest pain to the foot of the cross and leave it at His feet to be covered in forgiveness?

If you will give Him permission to access every part of your heart— the good, the bad, and the ugly—you will find freedom there.

Jesus, help me to open the places where my heart is hurting to You. I've carried this for so long it's become part of who I am and I'm afraid of who I will be if I give up my right to be angry. Lord, guide me closer to You and give me courage to allow You to bring healing and forgiveness to these hurts. Show me how to take one step closer to You each day. In Jesus' name. Amen.

Second Glance: Mark 15:1-5; Luke 23:1-16; John 18:28-38

Looking Beyond

The political climate of the day was complicated but it is crucial for understanding why both Jewish rulers and the Roman Governor put Jesus on trial.

The Romans ruled over the jurisdiction of Jerusalem, but they allowed the Jewish people to remain autonomous only to a certain extent so they could continue to operate under the law of Moses. However, the priests were careful to make sure they also obeyed the laws of the Romans, who reportedly revoked the right of the high council to sentence someone to death.

"So Pilate said to them, *'Take Him yourselves, and judge Him according to your law.' The Jews said to him, 'We are not permitted to put anyone to death.'*" John 28:31

The priests knew the Romans wouldn't care about their issues with Jesus proclaiming to be the Messiah, therefore they needed to bring charges that would get Pilate's attention. They needed to accuse Him of something the Romans would condemn. And they knew just what to claim—Jesus was a threat to Caesar by proclaiming to be King of the Jews.

Pilate questions Jesus and the crowd extensively, going back and forth between the courtyard where the Jewish people remained and inside where Jesus waited silently.

Pilate found no fault with Jesus and returned to the crowd once again. As the crowds shouted for blood, they mentioned Jesus was from Galilee. Hearing this, Pilate decided to send him to King Herod, who had jurisdiction over Galilee. It just so happened, Herod was in Jerusalem at the time, so the guards wasted no time moving Jesus.

Although Herod found no fault with Jesus either, he did attempt to humiliate the King of the Jews by adorning Him in a royal robe before sending Him back to Pilate.

During the entire ordeal, Jesus was silent—answering not one word for the accusations against Him.

Certainly Jesus was innocent, but we have to remember He was taking our place. We are the ones guilty of sin and sentenced to death. He silently stood before the judges, bearing the guilt that was not His, accepting the punishment not meant for Him.

As you read the other accounts of this event in the Scriptures today, take a few minutes to write out a prayer thanking Jesus for taking your place so you can have forgiveness and be reconciled with Him again.

THE DEATH SENTENCE

"Now at the feast he used to release for them any one prisoner whom they requested. The man named Barabbas had been imprisoned with the insurrectionists who had committed murder in the insurrection. The crowd went up and began asking him to do as he had been accustomed to do for them. Pilate answered them, saying, 'Do you want me to release for you the King of the Jews?' For he was aware that the chief priests had handed Him over because of envy. But the chief priests stirred up the crowd to ask him to release Barabbas for them instead. Answering again, Pilate said to them, 'Then what shall I do with Him whom you call the King of the Jews?' They shouted back, 'Crucify Him!' But Pilate said to them, 'Why, what evil has He done?' But they shouted all the more, 'Crucify Him!' Wishing to satisfy the crowd, Pilate released Barabbas for them, and after having Jesus scourged, he handed Him over to be crucified." Mark 15:6-15

"Crucify Him! Crucify Him!"

The crowd is chanting, demanding His blood. *"Let His blood be on us!"* Their chanting becomes the cry of one voice—the sinful voice of mankind.

Generation after generation of sin crying out, heard in the ears of the Creator who desperately wants to restore Himself with His creation.

Do you hear that one voice? That one familiar voice in the crowd? Don't you recognize it? It's your own voice.

Our spirit seeks to fill a God-shaped emptiness we don't understand, but our sinful hearts reject our Savior and joins the multitude.

"Crucify Him!"

Our sin demands His death, His sacrifice.

"Crucify Him!"

Jesus, the Lamb of God sent to take away our sin stands blameless, sinless, and holy; He speaks not one word—He simply allows us to defile Him with our hateful, murderous, sinful cries, and willingly wraps Himself in our sin and takes our place on the cross.

Our sin demands His death, His sacrifice, so He can redeem, restore, and reconnect us with the Father.

Jesus. Our Savior. Our Redeemer. Our Messiah.

The shadow grows larger, as Jesus takes His next steps towards the cross. What happens next will be hard to watch. But if we are to follow Him, we must witness this crucial part of His journey.

Second Glance: Matthew 27:15-26; Luke 23:18-25; John 18:38-40, 19:4-16

Looking Beyond

Pilate didn't want to give the death sentence. He found no fault in Jesus and had him beaten in the hopes of satisfying the Jewish leaders. But they weren't appeased, convinced Jesus was a liar who had blasphemed God, their law said that He should be put to death, and they wanted Him dead.

Jesus willingly wraps Himself in our sin & takes our place on the cross

Again Pilate cannot convince the Jewish leaders to reconsider. So in an attempt to show them the insignificance of Jesus as a threat, Pilate offers to free either Jesus or Barabbas, a murderer. Pilate was hoping they would choose Jesus but the crowd began to chant, "Crucify Him," and Pilate, fearing a riot, releases Barabbas and sentences Jesus to death.

Even as Jesus is standing in our place before the judge, He also takes Barabbas' place, quite literally. The Greek word for *release* is *Apoluo [ap-ol-oo'-o]* and means *to set free, acquit of a crime, release a debt.*

Barabbas doesn't know yet, but not only has he been set free from prison, but the One who takes his place, will make a way to release him of the debt of his sin.

These moments must be hard for Jesus. Imagine yourself in the corner of the courtyard, looking into His eyes. His body is sagging with the weight of the entire world on His shoulders, knowing what comes next will be much worse than watching His beloved children chanting for His death.

How does the idea that Jesus died so sinners, even murderers, could be saved deepen your views of God's mercy and grace?

What changes in your own life does God inspire you to make as you imagine yourself there in the crowd witnessing Jesus sentenced to crucifixion to bear the punishment for your sin?

Journal your thoughts as you read through the other gospel accounts listed in *Second Glance.*

day eighteen

JESUS IS BEATEN AND MOCKED

"..and after having Jesus scourged, [Pilate] handed Him over to be crucified. The soldiers took Him away into the palace (that is, the Praetorium), and they called together the whole Roman cohort. They dressed Him up in purple, and after twisting a crown of thorns, they put it on Him; and they began to acclaim Him, 'Hail, King of the Jews!' They kept beating His head with a reed, and spitting on Him, and kneeling and bowing before Him. After they had mocked Him, they took the purple robe off Him and put His own garments on Him. And they led Him out to crucify Him." Mark 15:15-20

As we linger in the dark shadows, let us watch the fullness of the suffering Jesus endures on our behalf.

Mockers spit in Jesus' face as they strip His clothes from His back. They relentlessly whip His bloody body over and over again until He becomes swollen and exhausted—barely recognizable. As their instruments of torture rip the flesh from His sides, Jesus' blood pools on the ground, soaking into the dry earth, fulfilling the prophecy in Isaiah.

Jesus endured the cross for YOU

"But He was pierced through for our transgressions, He was crushed for our iniquities; The chastening for our well-being fell upon Him, And by His scourging we are healed." Isaiah 53:5

Jesus looks into every eye and knows He does this for them. He sees their hearts, full of hate, greed, evil, and He loves them so much. His heart is full of compassion for the creation He has made. They are so precious to Him. They are beautiful in His sight because He knows their spirits could come alive if only they would believe in what He is doing now.

He wants so much to reach out and to hold them close. To tell them He loves them. But He remains silent and lets them have their way with Him. He knows He does this for them. He knows they need forgiveness the most. And this is the only way.

His flesh rips, but the searing pain is nothing compared to the breaking of His heart as the ones He so lovingly created shout hateful, vile words at Him. But just as He washed the disciples feet knowing they would betray and abandon Him, He also loves those in this crowd to the end. And the end is coming faster.

Jesus, thank You for enduring the suffering meant for me. Forgive me of the sin that sent You to the cross. Thank You for Your love even though I don't deserve it. Thank You for looking through time and seeing me—enduring the cross for me, so I could become alive in You and receive healing in my body. In Jesus' name. Amen.

Second Glance: Matthew 27:26-31; Luke 22:63-65; John 19:1-3; Isaiah 53:3-7

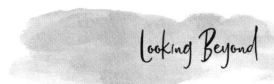
Looking Beyond

This part of the process of the cross is crucial as we watch our Savior being beaten and disfigured beyond recognition.

"His face was so disfigured he seemed hardly human, and from his appearance, one would scarcely know he was a man."
Isaiah 52:14 NLT

As Jesus' blood runs from His torn flesh, He covers our sin (also called atonement) as a fulfillment of the Old Testament requirement for sacrifice. The blood not only brings healing, but it covers the sin of mankind, extending forgiveness and reconciliation with God.

In Leviticus, God lays out specific, detailed instructions for the handling of sin offerings in a variety of different situations. But in each case, He required the killing of an animal so the priests could apply its blood to the altar.

That isn't the first time an animal was used to cover sin. In Genesis 3:21, God *"made garments of skin for Adam and his wife, and clothed them."* God has been providing a way to cover our sins since the very beginning.

God gave Moses laws to guide people away from sin, but they were difficult to remember and follow. One look at the book of Leviticus reveals His requirements nearly impossible to attain. Therefore, God established the sacrificial system to cover His people's wrongdoings and reconcile them to Himself until the time His Son would come as the final sacrifice. There is now no further need for priests to spill blood on an altar. Jesus fulfilled the sin sacrifice.

These are just a few connections between Old Testament sacrifices and Jesus' work at the cross. Take some time today to read through the other Gospel accounts and also the verses listed from Leviticus. See if you can find more ways the Old Testament sacrifices foreshadowed the details of Jesus crucifixion. Write them in your journal.

Read more about sin offering in the Old Testament:
Leviticus 4; 16:1-34

day nineteen

IT IS FINISHED

"So he [Pilate] then handed Him over to them to be crucified. They took Jesus, therefore, and He went out, bearing His own cross, to the place called the Place of a Skull, which is called in Hebrew, Golgotha. ...Therefore when Jesus had received the sour wine, He said, 'It is finished!' And He bowed His head and gave up His spirit."
John 19:16-17; 30

Standing at the foot of the cross, overshadowed by our Savior as He hangs between Heaven and hell—bloody and beaten beyond recognition—forsaken by the Father, Jesus looks down at us and says:

"It is finished."

No more sin.
No more separation from God.
No more eternal death

"It is finished."

No more guilt.
No more shame.
No more condemnation.
No more unforgiveness.

Every moment since the Garden of Eden has been a path leading to the cross

"It is finished. I have completed My purpose. I have taken your place. The price for your sin has been paid. The perfect sacrifice has been given; perfect blood has been shed."

His blood, meant to heal us and cover our sins, streams down His body and pools on the ground—Holy ground, where the Lamb of God is sacrificed.

Let's worship Him today.

Father, words can not give meaning to how undeserving I am of Your love and gift of eternal life. Thank You for loving me enough to give Your only Son so that I might be restored to You again. Jesus, Your sacrifice humbles me knowing You suffered the death that should have been mine. You, perfect and without sin, took the punishment for my sin and 'thank you' will never be enough. I bow before You today, in the shadow of Your cross, asking for forgiveness once again. Be my Savior and Lord every day of my life; help me to follow You. Thank you for the cross. In Jesus' name. Amen.

Second Glance: Matthew 27:32-54; Mark 15:21-39; Luke 23:26-47; John 19:16-37

Looking Beyond

As the darkness of the cross surrounds Him, Jesus knows death is next. Throughout the week, leading up to this moment, every bit of the human side of Jesus wanted to quit, wanted to give in, but the Divine pressed in closer, deeper, and loved more than He ever had.

His eyes gripped tight in pain, His burden growing heavier. The sin is overwhelming. His Father, holy and pure, can no longer look on our sin as it is wrapped tightly around His Son. And He turns His head.

Jesus' cry fills the air, *"Why have You forsaken Me?"* Jesus has never known the utter isolation He feels in this moment. Completely forsaken—just so we will never be forsaken, never know the complete isolation from God once we know Him as our Savior.

Jesus—a man from Galilee, sent from Heaven. Mary—His mother, torn as she watches the promised miracle being ripped and spilled out in front of her. She couldn't have imagined the details of this day as she held Him close as a babe.

Even in His last moments, Jesus makes sure Mary is cared for, because He is concerned about the details. He wants us to know He can handle the details of our lives, too.

He's been in the details since the very beginning, pointing us directly to this moment.

Scriptures from Genesis through to the Gospels foretell of Jesus' death and resurrection. The entire Bible points us to Him, to this moment, the biggest promise God has ever made—His Son, the fulfillment of the law, the sacrifice needed to forgive sin. Every moment since the Garden of Eden has pointed to this day. Every book, every chapter, every verse, has been a path leading to the cross.

The shadow began in the beginning with Adam and Eve and all of creation has been walking this path, closer to the Savior, waiting for this moment.

At the foot of the cross, staring up at our Savior, we are surrounded in complete darkness. The earth shakes violently as the Creator takes His last breath.

It is finished.

Jesus has fulfilled His purpose and has made the way to new life. The only thing standing in the way is our own selves. Will we believe in Him? Will we accept His story as our story? Will we draw closer to Him and ask for this free gift of love?

Today as you spend time in prayer, imagine yourself at the cross where Jesus has been crucified. Thank Him for this free gift of eternal life. Read the entire account of the cross in *Second Glance*, ask God to reveal new things about the cross as you read. Record any new insights you find in your journal.

THE SILENCE OF SATURDAY

"When it was evening, there came a rich man from Arimathea, named Joseph, who himself had also become a disciple of Jesus. This man went to Pilate and asked for the body of Jesus. Then Pilate ordered it to be given to him. And Joseph took the body and wrapped it in a clean linen cloth, and laid it in his own new tomb, which he had hewn out in the rock; and he rolled a large stone against the entrance of the tomb and went away. And Mary Magdalene was there, and the other Mary, sitting opposite the grave." Matthew 27:57-61

There they sit, in silence and grief. Their friend is gone. They feel the loss. The emptiness. The heaviness of the horrific sights of the previous day.

And the one person who can make it all better, who can comfort them? Gone. Dead. Buried.

There is silence.

No revelation of wisdom.
No parable tales to explain the events.
No words of comfort.
No looking into the face of God to search for signs of peace around the corners of His eyes.

Just a gaping, Jesus-shaped hole in their hearts—and deafening silence.

Oh, but what they did not know was just because they could not see Him, hear Him, touch Him, didn't mean He was quieted. He was at work behind the scenes; waging war on death and capturing the keys to the grave.

While they were grieving His passing, unsure of their present, He was securing their eternity. He was completing the plan He had for them—and for us.

He wasn't worried about His friends' momentary worry, fear, or doubt. He had already prepared them for this. He knew they would feel this way, so He had spent much time giving them the words they would need to carry them through the quiet.

When the silence of Saturday surrounds your heart and you can't hear His voice, remember He is still working for your eternal good.

He has prepared you for the days of silence. You already have His promises found in His Word.

You already know victory is coming.

With shouts of joy and tears of gladness—Sunday is coming!

Lord, it's hard for me when it feels like You are silent. Help me to remember You are still working behind the scenes, You haven't for-gotten me. Even if I all I hear is silence, remind me You still see me and hear my prayers. Help me to hold on to the promises You have written in Scripture. Thank you Jesus for giving me Your Word to comfort me through these hard times. In Jesus' name. Amen.

Second Glance: Mark 15:42-47; Luke 23:50-56; John 19:38-42; Revelation 1:18

Looking Beyond

I don't know about you, but some of the hardest times I have faced are when God seemed silent. I remember going through cancer treatments and felt like no matter how much I prayed, I just couldn't hear His voice. However, the one thing I knew for certain was if I wanted to know what He had to say, then I would have to open up the Bible and read—because the Scriptures are His words to us.

While they were grieving His passing, unsure of their present, He was securing their eternity

As I took my Bible in one hand and my phone in my other hand, I began to search for verses online that spoke to my specific circumstances for healing, strength, life, and comfort. As I found those verses in my Bible, I marked them, then wrote them in my journal so I could read them on days when I was too weak to pick up my heavy Bible.

Maybe what you are facing isn't a health crisis but different circumstances that seem overwhelming, and you feel God is silent. Remember: He has already given you His promises in His Word, all you have to do is find it, pray it, and then trust He is working on your behalf.

Spend time today reflecting on where you feel God is silent and then use a Bible concordance or search engine to find verses that speak to your circumstances. Mark them in your Bible and write them down to remind yourself that He sees and hears you and His promises are for you.

HE IS ALIVE

"When the Sabbath was over, Mary Magdalene, and Mary the mother of James, and Salome, bought spices, so that they might come and anoint Him. Very early on the first day of the week, they came to the tomb when the sun had risen. They were saying to one another, 'Who will roll away the stone for us from the entrance of the tomb?' Looking up, they saw that the stone had been rolled away, although it was extremely large. Entering the tomb, they saw a young man sitting at the right, wearing a white robe; and they were amazed. And he said to them, 'Do not be amazed; you are looking for Jesus the Nazarene, who has been crucified. He has risen; He is not here; behold, here is the place where they laid Him. But go, tell His disciples and Peter, "He is going ahead of you to Galilee; there you will see Him, just as He told you."'" Mark 16:1-7

Sunrise after the Sabbath, the first day of the week, heavy-hearted and grieving, Mary Magdalene and a group of women make their way toward the burial place of their Friend.

(insert your name)
I love you enough to die for you -Jesus

They plan to anoint His body and fully expect to find it. But instead of the body of their Friend, they find an empty tomb. They are startled and frightened.

The angel proclaims, "He is Risen!"

The women are charged with the important task to deliver the news to the disciples and Peter.

Mary immediately runs to tell Peter and John of the empty tomb. Together with Mary, they race back to the garden and find...nothing. No body. No Friend. Just an empty grave and some burial linens.

The disciples return home and leave Mary—alone and weeping.

"But Mary was standing outside the tomb weeping... Jesus said to her, 'Woman, why are you weeping? Whom are you seeking?' Supposing Him to be the gardener, she said to Him, 'Sir, if you have carried Him away, tell me where you have laid Him, and I will take Him away.' Jesus said to her, 'Mary!' She turned and said to Him in Hebrew, 'Rabboni!' (which means, Teacher)." John 20:11, 15-16

As Mary stands looking into an empty tomb, a man captures her attention. She thinks He is the gardener and inquires where Her Lord has been taken.

One word—"Mary."

Immediately she knows; she knows the voice of her Teacher, her Friend, her Savior—Jesus!

Easter Sunday not only brings the good news of Jesus' resurrection, but it also delivers the message of salvation from a God who knows your name, too.

"Before I formed you in the womb I knew you, And before you were born I consecrated you." Jeremiah 1:5

He knew your sins and He sent His only Son to suffer and die on the cross anyway. Why? Because He deeply loves you.

"But God demonstrates His own love toward us, in that while we were yet sinners, Christ died for us." Romans 5:8

If you have never asked Christ to forgive you and to be part of your life, why not do so today? I would love to pray with you.

Even if you've been a Christian as long as you can remember, you'll benefit from reminding yourself of the simple beginnings of your faith.

Jesus, I believe You are the Son of God sent to die for my sins. I believe You forgive me and restore my relationship with You. Lord, I want You to be part of my life, helping me to make the best decisions and live for You. Jesus, thank You for the cross and the resurrection, making it possible for me to have life with You forever. In Jesus' name. Amen.

Second Glance: Matthew 28:1-10; Mark 16:1-8; Luke 24:1-12; John 20:1-18

Looking Beyond

Not only did Jesus speak Mary's name, but notice in Mark 16:7 the angel charges Mary to go tell *"the disciples and Peter."*

Only God could have known the inner feelings Peter had about his denial of Jesus and his grief over losing his closest Friend. What depths of sorrow and regret Peter must be experiencing—He might have thought, "Surely God would never want to speak with me again. I have failed Him. What a loser I am." Yet God made a specific request through His angelic messenger, *"Go tell the disciples and Peter."*

Mary might have thought, "Peter?! Peter? You mean the one who, just hours before, denied he even knew the Son of God? Are you sure, God?"

Yes. Even Peter. His sins were covered at the cross, too. And, Jesus had some restoration in store for Peter. (See John 21)

Peter is changed by the resurrection and the Holy Spirit and he teaches why it was important for Jesus to be resurrected during his sermon in Acts: *"...this Man, delivered over by the predetermined plan and foreknowledge of God, you nailed to a cross by the hands of godless men and put Him to death. But God raised Him up again, putting an end to the agony of death, since it was impossible for Him to be held in its power."*

"...Therefore let all the house of Israel know for certain that God has made Him both Lord and Christ—this Jesus whom you crucified." Acts 22:23-24, 36

The resurrection is the cornerstone of our faith. His resurrection is proof He is the Son of God and therefore, He is indeed the Christ, the

One who brings forgiveness and the hope of eternal life with Him.

Celebrate His resurrection today. Rejoice knowing that He has come to forgive you and give you everlasting life with Him. May you, like Mary, hear His voice as He calls your name:

" {insert your name} I love you enough to die for you."
  ~ Jesus

Beyond the Shadow

We have journeyed a long way since beginning this study twenty-one days ago. We've walked together in the shadow of the cross, learning from Jesus in His last days. We've found freedom beyond the shadow of sin He offers us through His sacrifice, where we can now walk in the light of His forgiveness. No matter whether you fell deeper in love with Jesus, or you discovered His everlasting love for you for the first time over these last three weeks, you may find yourself asking, "Now what? I've come all this way. What do I do next?"

The disciples felt the same way as they gathered together behind closed doors, went out on fishing boats to work, and traveled to other towns, trying to figure out, "What next?"

And then Jesus showed up.

> *"During the forty days after he suffered and died,*
> *he appeared to the apostles from time to time,*
> *and he proved to them in many ways that he was actually alive.*
> *And he talked to them about the Kingdom of God."*
> Acts 1:3 NLT

Over a period of 40 days, He walked with them on the road to Emmaus, ate breakfast with them on the shore of Galilee, explained Scripture, and talked about the Kingdom of God.

Right before Jesus ascended to Heaven, He had a few last words for those who would follow Him.

"And Jesus came up and spoke to them, saying, 'All authority has been given to Me in heaven and on earth. Go therefore and make disciples of all the nations, baptizing them in the name of the Father and the Son and the Holy Spirit, teaching them to observe all that I commanded you; and lo, I am with you always, even to the end of the age.'" Matthew 28:18-20

This may be the end of Jesus' journey to the cross, but our journey beyond its shadow is just beginning. And Jesus, Himself, sends us out and cheers us on with the same words, "Go, tell others."

Share the good news of Jesus with your family, friends, neighbors... everyone! Tell them about the journey you've been on and how much Jesus loves them, too!

Not sure how to share Jesus with others?

- Invite a friend to coffee and tell them about what you have been reading over the last 21 days.
- Start a small Bible study in your home, office, or church. Feel free to use this book as your guide.
- Use the resources & social media posts at Real Women Ministries to share with your friends.
- Become involved in outreach events in your church or community.

The best way to share Jesus with others is to just do it! Say a prayer asking God to make you aware of the people He puts in your path who need to hear about Him. Ask Him to fill you with His wisdom and compassion as you share what He has been doing in your life. Invite them to journey alongside you beyond the shadow of the cross.

Lord, thank You for all the ways You have shown me Your goodness and love, especially over the past few weeks. I want to be obedient to tell others about You, so help me to be aware of the people I encounter throughout the week that need to hear about Your love. Help me to be brave and courageous as I continue to follow You.
In Jesus' name. Amen.

Acknowledgements

To my husband, **Rick**—You had no idea seven years ago when you surprised me with my first blog site how much I loved to write. Although your desire was to make communication with friends and family easier for me through a difficult season of cancer treatments, what you truly gave me was the gift of rediscovering my love of words. Thank you for supporting my writing even though it means some nights I slip into bed after midnight or begin my day at 3 am. You never ask one question when you come home and I'm still in my PJ's with crazy hair. And when I looked at you across the aisle of the plane and said, "I just did something crazy. I sent an email committing to write a book," your response was, "It's about time." Thank you for believing in me and loving me through good & bad and sickness & health—I can't wait to grow old with you.

To my kids, **Camilla** and **Joshua**—Even though I was nervous to tell people I was writing a book, both of you encouraged me and said you believed in me. You'll never know how much that means to have my kids cheering me on. I am blessed to be your mom and nothing has made me happier than to see you become such amazing adults. You make me proud. To my bonus kids, **Samantha** and **Mason**, thank you for loving my kids and being part of our family.

To my friend, **Debbie Myers**—The truth is, this book wouldn't have happened without you. Your prayers covered me every day as I struggled with words and deadlines and insecurities. Only you know how many tears have birthed this book, and you have shed them all with me. Who could have known after 25 years Gertie and Marge would still be sipping coffee, sharing the Word, and laughing and crying through it all? Our friendship has challenged me, pushed me, and blessed me more than I could have ever imagined. Thanks for taking the ride with me.

To my designer, **Jana Kennedy-Spicer**—Your amazing creativity and graphic design skills have made this book more than I could have ever dreamed. Without your hard work, truly this book would never have happened. I am so privileged to be able to work with you and even more blessed to call you friend.

To my editor, **Liz Giertz**—What a gift you have been to me. There is no doubt in my mind God looked down on the Embassy Suites that day and said, "These two girls need to meet." Your unfailing encouragement pushes me to continue writing. You have been my labor coach as we birthed these words together through your amazing editing skills. And as I said before, you have made me sound so much smarter than I really am. Thank you for all the hard work and putting up with my crazy late-night text messages. I am going to miss working together everyday...maybe I better get started on that next book?!

To my online community at **Real Women Ministries**—Thank you for faithfully showing up to encourage each other in God's Word, to pray for one another, and for supporting me. I pray God continues to grow our community as we follow after Him.

In The Shadow Of The Cross

Scripture Reading List

Day One
Matthew 16:24-25
Mark 8:34-35
Luke 9:23-24

Day Two
Matthew 26:6-13
Mark 14:3-9
John 12:1-8

Day Three
Matthew 21:1-11
Mark 11:1-10
Luke 19:28-40
John 12:12-15

Day Four
Luke 19:41-44

Day Five
Matthew 26:1-5
Mark 14:1-2
Luke 22:1-2
John 11:47-57

Day Six
Matthew 26:14-16
Mark 14:10-11
Luke 22:3-6

Day Seven
Luke 22:7-13
Matthew 26:17-19
Mark 14:12-16

Day Eight
John 13:1-17

Day Nine
Matthew 26:20-25
Mark 14:17-21
John 13:18-30

Day Ten
Matthew 26:26-29
Mark 14:22-25
Luke 22:14-20

Day Eleven
Matthew 26:31-35
Mark 14:26-31
Luke 22:31-34
John 13:36-38

Day Twelve
Matthew 26:36-46
Luke 22:39-46
Mark 14:32-42

Day Thirteen
Matthew 26:47-56
Mark 14:43-50
Luke 22:47-53

Day Fourteen
Matthew 26:57-68
Mark 14:53-65
Luke 22:66-71
John 18:19-24

Day Fifteen
Matthew 26:69-75
Mark 14:66-72
Luke 22:55-62
John 18:15-18;
25-27

Day Sixteen
Matthew 27:11-14
Mark 15:1-5
Luke 23:1-16
John 18:28-38

Day Seventeen
Matthew 27:15-26
Mark 15:6-15
Luke 23:18-25
John 18:38-40;
19:4-16

Day Eighteen
Matthew 27:26-31
Mark 15:15-20
Luke 22:63-65
John 19:1-3

Day Nineteen
Matthew 27:32-54
Mark 15:21-39
Luke 23:26-47
John 19:16-37

Day Twenty
Matthew 27:57-61
Mark 15:42-47
Luke 23:50-56
John 19:38-42

Day Twenty-One
Matthew 28:1-10
Mark 16:1-8
Luke 24:1-12
John 20:1-18

Stephanie K. Adams

Meet the Author

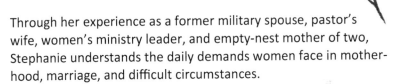

Stephanie K. Adams is a writer and founder of Real Women Ministries, where a community of women gather to grow their relationship with each other and God through encouragement and accountability to studying the Bible, and cultivating a love for His Word.

Through her experience as a former military spouse, pastor's wife, women's ministry leader, and empty-nest mother of two, Stephanie understands the daily demands women face in motherhood, marriage, and difficult circumstances.

After her diagnosis of an aggressive breast cancer, Stephanie began writing about her faith journey through treatments, and ultimately, God's miraculous healing. Stephanie continues to write about God's faithfulness to encourage other women facing real life issues.

Stephanie is a contributing author to *Bearing Fruit: Living Rooted in Christ.* Her writing has also been featured on *Faithfully Following Ministries, The Blythe Daniel Agency's Blog About, Triple Negative Breast Cancer Foundation* and more.

Stephanie is married to her high school sweetheart, Rick. They have two adult children and their spouses, as well as their fur-babies, Maggie and Obi. Stephanie enjoys reading, a good cup of coffee, and Saturday breakfast with her husband.

To join a community of real women sharing real life together, visit www.RealWomenMinistries.org

You can also connect with Stephanie on social media:
Facebook: www.facebook.com/realwomenministries
Instagram: www.instagram.com/realwomenministries

Resources

Additional *In The Shadow of the Cross* Resources include:

Daily Scripture Reading List
Study Journal
Phone Lock Screens

To download, visit
www.RealWomenMinistries.org/ShadowOfTheCross

Resources

We all have spiritual roots extending outward and returning food for our soul. The question is – what is our life source? What are we feeding on?

Are we feeding on the fresh flowing life giving waters that a healthy relationship with God offers? Or the stale, stagnant, dirty waters of the world? It's our choice, you see.

In this four part Bible Study, we'll learn about the key to living a fruit bearing life – living rooted in Christ.

For more information, visit:
www.SweetToTheSoul.com/bearing-fruit

Made in the USA
Columbia, SC
13 March 2019